21st
Century
Skills Library

COOL MILITARY CAREERS

MOTOR TRANSPORT OPERATOR

WIL MARA

Published in the United States of America by
Cherry Lake Publishing, Ann Arbor, Michigan
www.cherrylakepublishing.com

Content Adviser
Cynthia Watson, PhD, author of *U.S. National Security*

Credits
Cover and page 1, ©Arthur Eugene Preston/Shutterstock, Inc.; page 4, U.S. Army photo by Spc.
David A. Waters/Released; page 6, U.S. Marine Corps photo by Gunnery Sgt. J.L. Wright Jr./Released;
page 9, Official U.S. Marine Corps photo by Lance Cpl. Maxton G. Musselman/Released; page 10,
U.S. Marine Corps photo by Staff Sgt. Luis R. Agostini/Released; pages 12 and 22, U.S. Marine
Corps photo by Cpl. Casey Tomlinson/Released; page 14, U.S. Air Force photo by Staff Sgt. Stephen
Schester/Released; page 15, U.S. Army photo by Sgt. Frank Sanchez III/Released; page 17, U.S.
Marine Corps photo by Sgt. Rebekka Heite/Released; page 18, U.S. Marine Corps photo by Sergeant
Justin Par/Released; page 20, U.S. Marine Corps photo by Lance Cpl. John M. McCall/Released;
page 24, U.S. Marine Corps photo by Sgt. Mallory S. VanderSchans/Released; page 26, U.S. Army
photo by Sgt. Karl Williams/Released; page 27, U.S. Army photo by Sgt. Andy Mehler/Released;
page 28, ©Monkey Business Images/Shutterstock, Inc.

Library of Congress Cataloging-in-Publication Data
Mara, Wil.
  Motor transport operator/by Wil Mara.
     p. cm.—(Cool military careers) (21st century skills library)
  Includes bibliographical references and index.
  Audience: Grades 4-6.
  ISBN 978-1-61080-450-9 (lib. bdg.) — ISBN 978-1-61080-537-7 (e-book) —
ISBN 978-1-61080-624-4 (pbk.)
  1. Military trucks—United States--Juvenile literature. 2. Truck drivers—United States—
Juvenile literature. 3. United States—Armed Forces—Vocational guidance—Juvenile literature.
I. Title.
  UG618.M37 2012
  355.3'4—dc23   2012003754

Cherry Lake Publishing would like to acknowledge
the work of The Partnership for 21st Century Skills.
Please visit *www.21stcenturyskills.org* for more information.

Printed in the United States of America
Corporate Graphics Inc.
July 2012
CLFA11

TABLE OF CONTENTS

MOTOR TRANSPORT OPERATOR

CHAPTER ONE
ON THE ROAD AGAIN

Brian is more nervous than he's ever been. He's driving a truck the size of a school bus, bouncing along a winding dirt road thousands of miles from home. There is

Motor transport operators drive huge trucks that carry critical supplies, often during dangerous military missions.

rough, rugged **terrain** all around, dotted with jagged rocks and weedy bushes. A line of mountains looms in the distance.

Up ahead, just beyond a dusty rise in the road, he sees black smoke billowing into the sky. The air is filled with the sound of chattering machine guns and exploding bombs. All of this frightens him, but it also makes him more determined to do his job. He knows there's a fierce battle unfolding and that the men and women on his side need his help. In fact, they might not win this one without him.

Brian floors the gas pedal, the engine roars, and the truck lurches forward. He is moving incredibly fast. He reaches the top of the rise and begins rumbling down the other side. His heart pounds harder and faster when he sees the scene in the valley below. There are tanks and helicopters, and people in uniforms and helmets running everywhere. The smoke is thicker now, pierced by bright flashes of gunfire. There is much yelling and screaming.

Brian screeches to a halt at base camp, and a crew swarms around the truck. As he climbs down from the driver's seat, he salutes the officer in charge. Then Brian goes to the back of the truck and drops the gate so the others can see the precious **cargo** he's brought: food, water, medical equipment for the wounded, and lots of **ammunition**. Everyone cheers and pats him on the back, and then he begins helping them unload. They might just win this one after all.

■ ■ ■

Do you like the idea of being behind the wheel of a big, powerful vehicle? If so, then becoming a motor transport operator (MTO) in the military might be a good career choice for you. The job of an MTO is to move cargo from one place to another. You won't often have to do this in a situation as dangerous as the one above, but there may be times when you do. You will be responsible for the safety

MTOs transport everything from advanced weaponry to soldiers' mail.

and security of the load you carry and for the upkeep of the vehicle you command.

The U.S. military has used wheeled vehicles since the Revolutionary War (1775–1783), when supplies were moved around on wagons pulled by people or animals. During the American Civil War (1861–1865), wounded soldiers were often carried off battlefields in carts. In World War II (1939–1945), more than 35 million American soldiers and 120 million tons of supplies were transported to the places where they were needed the most.

 LIFE & CAREER SKILLS

Motor transport operators learn about more than just trucks during their term of service. They learn how to think quickly to handle challenging situations, how to manage details and utilize organizational skills, and how to focus on a goal until it is reached. These are the types of life skills that make them better soldiers and better people. These skills contribute to their personal growth and maturity, and will prove highly valuable along the road of life.

Today, the U.S. military has more than 50,000 trucks and other wheeled transport vehicles. They come in all shapes and sizes and are used for a wide variety of purposes. Tanker trucks are used to transport water and fuel, and long trailers move tons of supplies. There are also troop transports, heavy-equipment carriers, and medical and passenger buses. These are specially made vehicles—you won't find any of these at your local car dealership!

The importance of wheeled vehicles in the military, and the people who know how to use them, is enormous. Military units have to be able to swing into action at a moment's notice. This means moving not just the soldiers on the ground but also their weapons, ammunition, food, medical supplies, and clothing. Do you think you could handle such an awesome responsibility?

MTOs help keep military
operations running smoothly.

CHAPTER TWO
GETTING THE JOB

To become a motor transport operator, you must join the military. The branches of the military, also called the armed forces, are the U.S. Army, Navy, Air Force, Marines, and Coast

All branches of the military need MTOs to help transport cargo.

Guard. The mission of the military is to protect and defend the United States. As a member of the military, you will be helping to do this.

You must be at least 18 years old before you can join (or 17, if you have permission from your parents or legal guardians). You have to be a U.S. citizen, which means you were either born in the United States or born in another country and have become a legal U.S. citizen. Even if you meet these two requirements, you can still be turned down. For example, you cannot join the military if you are a single parent. You cannot owe a large amount of money to banks or businesses. You should not have a criminal record or a history of drug or alcohol problems. There are also height requirements. Generally, you must be taller than 60 inches (152 centimeters) but shorter than 80 inches (203 cm).

Once you join, you will take several tests. Some will determine your physical condition. Others are designed to get inside your mind so the military can get some idea of who you are. They want to make sure you're the kind of person who is good at taking orders and following commands. They also want to see if you're better at working as part of a team or working by yourself. They will try to determine your weaknesses as well as your strengths. Even if you've asked for a specific job, they might decide that you're better suited for something different.

To become a motor transport operator, you should have an interest in driving as well as natural **mechanical** ability. If you're not the type of person who is good at taking things apart and putting them back together, then this probably isn't the right job for you. You should also be responsible, meaning you're the kind of person who can be trusted to carry out a plan and get it done right. Being organized helps, since you'll

MTOs need mechanical skills to repair their vehicles in case of breakdowns.

be expected to handle many small details and do some paperwork.

A motor transport operator has to lift cargo on and off a vehicle almost every day, so having a strong, healthy body is important. You'll also need to have normal **color perception**, because some of your tasks will involve color-coding. If you have breathing or heart conditions, you probably wouldn't be considered for this kind of work.

LEARNING & INNOVATION SKILLS

Basic training is the physical and mental preparation that all new military recruits are required to undergo immediately after they've joined the service. Some people say it is more like torture than anything else. It is designed to get you into the proper mental and physical condition, and it is an indicator of whether or not you can handle the challenges that lie ahead. The military stresses the importance of finishing all tasks that you start. This is a good habit to develop not only for your military service but also for the rest of your life.

You should have a driver's license and, eventually, a special license for the exact type of vehicle you'll be driving. You probably will not be required to qualify for high **security clearance**. Most of the cargo you'll be transporting will not be top secret, nor will the vehicles have cutting-edge technology. There are a few motor transport operators, however, who do require special clearance. These are usually people who

Most MTOs spend their time carrying everyday military supplies such as ammunition.

More experienced MTOs are tasked with transporting sensitive materials.

have been in the service for a long time and whose backgrounds have been thoroughly investigated. These individuals have earned their superiors' trust. Also, most MTOs are enlisted personnel, rather than officers, and have only a high school education rather than a college degree.

All new military recruits are required to go through a period of basic combat training, which lasts about 10 weeks. Future motor transport operators undergo another seven weeks of training (depending on which branch of the military they are in) specifically for their MTO position. This training includes lessons in proper operation and maintenance of various vehicles and accident-prevention techniques. Trainees are also taught safety procedures for the transportation of hazardous and dangerous materials, record-keeping procedures, and safety checks. Some of this training takes place in a classroom, but much of it is hands-on, either in the field or on a **simulator**. Before you are entrusted with your own rig, you have to log more than 200 hours of training time in an actual vehicle!

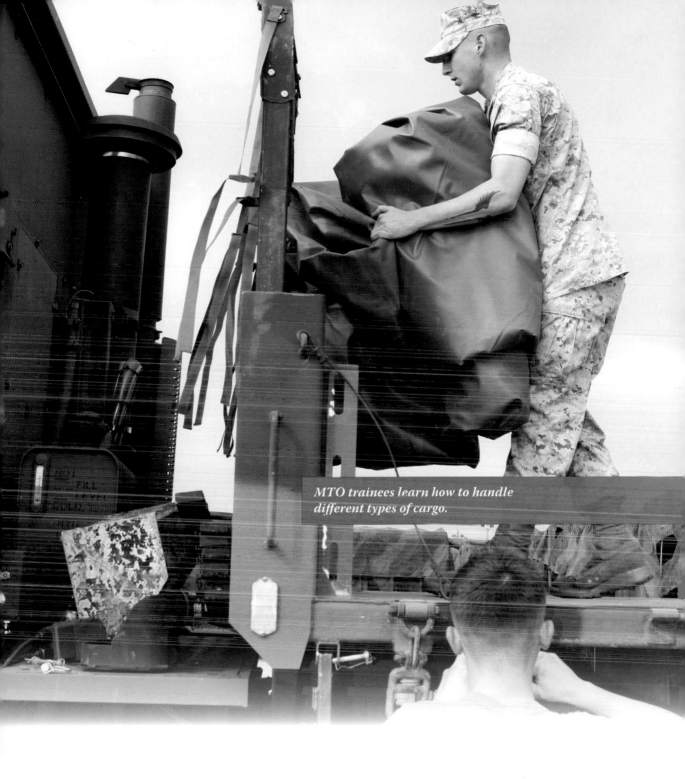

MTO trainees learn how to handle different types of cargo.

CHAPTER THREE
LIFE BEHIND THE WHEEL

As a motor transport operator, you'll lead a very busy life. You could be called to duty day or night. And when you're not on the road, you'll be spending much of your time making sure your vehicles are in good shape and ready to roll.

MTOs use maps to help them plan routes through unfamiliar areas.

One of your primary functions will be to drive a vehicle from one location to another. Often this will be a relatively simple task, such as when you have to transport cargo within the United States. Other times, you'll face difficult challenges such as driving on rough terrain or in areas where there are no roads. You might also be called on to drive in bad weather and in battle conditions where an enemy might attack your vehicle. There will also be instances when you have to operate a vehicle after only a few hours of sleep, which means you'll have to focus your attention regardless of how tired you are.

During your journeys, you will be expected to operate equipment critical to your duties. Military vehicles are equipped with high-tech communication devices, advanced navigation systems, and onboard computers. This equipment will provide you with constantly updated information about your objectives, which is crucial since your assignment could change at a moment's notice. You will also need to keep an eye on the equipment that monitors the health of your vehicle. If there is a problem with the engine, for example, you'll want to know about it as soon as possible.

You will be responsible not just for the safe transport of your cargo but also for the cargo itself. You will receive a list of every item in your care, and you will have to make sure each one is accounted for, on board, and in good condition. You will need to check this list when you first receive

the cargo and again when you arrive at your destination. You
will need to make sure all items are securely fastened and in
place before you start your journey. If certain items are too
heavy to be lifted by hand, it's still your job to make sure that
they are properly loaded and unloaded from your vehicle. You
may have to operate a forklift or other piece of equipment to
handle the material.

There may be times when your vehicle comes under attack
by enemy forces. Most military vehicles are equipped with

*Most MTOs are required to carry weapons
and are trained for combat.*

some form of weaponry. In these situations, you will have to man those weapons to defend not just yourself but your cargo. It's very common to attack a military's source of supplies. Think about it—how can soldiers continue fighting if they run out of essential supplies such as food, water, gasoline, or ammunition?

LIFE & CAREER SKILLS

There are times when a motor transport operator is part of a **convoy**. A convoy is a group of vehicles that travel together. Perhaps 200 soldiers need to go from one base to another, but one vehicle carries only 50. In that case, a convoy of four vehicles is required. MTOs need to keep in contact with the other drivers, although one person is in charge of the convoy overall. In a battlefield situation, there are special techniques for defending a convoy if it is attacked. Being part of a convoy teaches you how to work as a team, how to depend on others, and how others depend on you. A group of people working together can almost always achieve much more than one person working alone.

If you are part of a medical unit, you will probably spend some time transporting soldiers who have been injured during battle. Bringing wounded soldiers to a hospital for emergency medical care is one of the most important duties a motor transport operator has during wartime. Drivers of such vehicles may also need to perform emergency medical procedures from time to time.

Maintenance is a big part of an MTO's job.

When you're not on the road, you will spend a lot of time making sure your vehicle is in good operating condition. You will check fluid levels and air pressure in the tires. You will be under the hood and beneath the **chassis**, looking for leaks and changing worn or broken parts. You will be required to keep a detailed set of logs, which will include not just mechanical work but also time spent on the road, miles driven, and the amount of fuel used.

If your vehicle experiences mechanical problems while driving, you will have to either make the repairs on the spot or call for assistance. There will be times when your vehicle will *become* cargo itself and will have to be transported to another location. This might happen during wartime, when your vehicle is sent to a foreign country. When that happens, you'll be responsible for preparing it for the trip.

CHAPTER FOUR
THE ROAD AHEAD

I t's impossible to say how many motor transport operator positions will be available in the military in the future. The

The military will always need skilled, responsible people to drive its vehicles.

military's needs vary, based on factors such as whether the nation is at war or how much money the military receives from the government. If there are no MTO positions available, you may have to put your name on a waiting list. You can still join the military, however, and take another job while you wait for an opening.

Being a member of the military has many advantages regardless of what position you hold. All training you receive is free of charge. As a **civilian**, you usually have to pay for career training. If you are a member of the military and decide to go to college, the military will pay your education costs. You are then required, however, to serve in the military for a certain amount of time.

A member of the military also receives free food, clothing, medical care, and a place to live. If you're lucky, you might be assigned to an interesting location in a distant part of the world. And if you stay in the military long enough, you'll receive retirement benefits.

You also receive a salary as a motor transport operator. Your pay in the military is based on your **rank** and the number of years you've served. For example, a private who enlisted only recently will make very little in comparison to a general who has served all his or her life. The average MTO makes somewhere in the range of $35,000 per year. As time goes on and you gain more experience, your salary increases. Salaries also vary in each branch of the service and can be affected by how badly the military needs MTOs at any given moment.

Many of the skills you learn as an MTO can help you find a similar job once you leave the military. There are literally millions of cargo vehicles on the roads every day. Just about every company that produces goods has a need to ship them from one place to another. You could work in the trucking industry, or you could drive a bus.

Driving a military cargo truck is very similar to driving a civilian cargo truck.

People who have served in the military make excellent workers when they return to civilian life.

With your experience managing cargo and handling on-the-road emergency situations, you'll be more desirable to an employer. Many businesses prefer to hire former military people over nonmilitary people because ex-military workers often have more discipline, focus, and sense of responsibility. With your military MTO experience, you could also seek a management position, where you would be overseeing a transport operation rather than doing the actual driving, loading, and unloading.

Driving skills come in handy in many civilian jobs.

The U.S. military is always in need of talented, dedicated individuals to move troops and other cargo from place to place. The military offers many benefits and opportunities that you cannot find anywhere else. If you have a passion for wheeled vehicles and some basic organizational skills, perhaps a career as a motor transport operator is in your future!

GLOSSARY

ammunition (am-yuh-NISH-uhn) objects, such as bullets or shells, that are fired from weapons

basic training (BAY-sik TRAYN-ing) a period of mental and physical preparation that readies a person for a career in the military

cargo (KAHR-goh) freight that is carried by any vehicle

chassis (CHAS-ee) the frame of a vehicle

civilian (suh-VIL-yuhn) not part of the armed forces

color perception (KUHL-ur pur-SEP-shuhn) the ability to see colors

convoy (KAHN-voi) a group of vehicles that travel together for safety and convenience

mechanical (mih-KAN-i-kuhl) having to do with machines or engines

rank (RANGK) official job level or position

security clearance (si-KYOOR-i-tee KLEER-uhns) the status of a person in regard to how much access to secret information they are allowed

simulator (SIM-yuh-lay-tur) a machine that trains a person to perform a task, such as driving a truck, by imitating the conditions and controls

terrain (tuh-RAYN) the surface features of an area of land

FOR MORE INFORMATION

BOOKS

Ellis, Catherine. *Cars and Trucks*. New York: PowerKids Press, 2007.

Gonzalez, Lissette. *The U.S. Military: Defending the Nation*. New York: PowerKids Press, 2008.

Harasymiw, Mark A. *Army*. New York: Gareth Stevens, 2011.

WEB SITES

Military Careers
www.militarycareersinfo.com
Check out this site to learn more about different jobs in the military, the various branches of the military, and the advantages and disadvantages of military service.

Today's Military
www.todaysmilitary.com
This site provides lots of valuable information about the opportunities and benefits each branch of the U.S. military offers, so that you can make an informed choice about joining the armed forces.

U.S. Army—Careers & Jobs: Motor Transport Operator
*www.goarmy.com/careers-and-jobs/browse-career-and-job
-categories/transportation-and-aviation/motor-transport
-operator.html*
This site offers a complete overview of a career as an MTO, including information on job duties, salary, training, education benefits, and future civilian careers.

INDEX

ABOUT THE AUTHOR

Wil Mara is the award-winning author of more than 120 books, many of which are educational titles for young readers. Information about his work can be found at www.wilmara.com.